SOUPS, S[...] AND SNACKS

Caroline Ellwood

🦅 GOLDEN PRESS / NEW YORK
Western Publishing Company, Inc.
Racine, Wisconsin

CONTENTS

NOTES:

See pages 6–7 for basic soup stocks and garnishing suggestions.

Always preheat the oven to the specified temperature.

Margarine can be substituted for butter in all recipes.

If substituting dried herbs for fresh, use a third of the amount;
if substituting fresh for dried, use 3 times the amount.

This edition prepared under the supervision of
Joanna Morris

This edition published 1984 by Golden Press
Library of Congress Catalog Card Number: 84-80334
ISBN 0-307-09969-5
Golden® and Golden Press® are registered trademarks
of Western Publishing Company, Inc.

First published in the U.K. by Cathay Books,
59 Grosvenor Steet, London W1

Printed in Hong Kong

INTRODUCTION

There are often times when a regular meal is just too much food. The recipes in this book offer the opportunity to create the kind of meal you want. Combine soup and a sandwich, perhaps a light fruit salad and crackers, or maybe a quiche with a cold vegetable salad.

First, there is a selection of hot and cold soups. And what could be more versatile than soup? In a cup, it's a snack; in a bowl, it's a mini-meal. Best of all, most soups are quick and easy to prepare and many can be made in advance and frozen.

Salads, too, offer many options. They can stand on their own or team up with soup or a sandwich, depending on the occasion. It's a good idea to keep salad fixings and dressings on hand for the quickest of quick snacks.

Finally, when you're looking for a heartier snack, try egg and cheese dishes—omelets are wonderful for lunch or a late supper. Homemade pizza is a nice change of pace after tennis or golf, and sandwiches with extra "decks" are always welcome.

The only thing difficult about this cookbook is choosing what to serve.

Chicken Stock

4 lb chicken backs and necks
4 quarts water
2 onions, chopped
4 carrots, chopped
1 leek, chopped
3 stalks celery, chopped
Bouquet garni

Combine the chicken and water in a deep pot and bring to a boil. Skim thoroughly and add the remaining ingredients. Simmer, uncovered, for about 4 hours.

Strain the stock and cool. Refrigerate and use as needed, reboiling every 3 days; skim before using. Or freeze until required.

Makes about 3 quarts

Beef Stock

4 lb beef bones
4 quarts water
2 large onions, chopped
3 carrots, chopped
2 stalks celery, chopped
1 clove garlic, sliced
Bouquet garni

Spread the bones out in a large roasting pan and cook in a 350° oven until browned.

Transfer the bones to a deep pot and add the water. Bring to a boil and skim thoroughly. Add the remaining ingredients and simmer for 4 hours.

Strain the stock and cool. Refrigerate and use as needed, reboiling every 3 days; skim before using. Or freeze until required.

Makes about 3 quarts

Fish Stock

1 lb fish bones and heads
1 onion, chopped
2 leeks, chopped
Bouquet garni
1 cup dry white wine

Place the fish, onion and leeks in a deep pot. Add the bouquet garni and wine; add water to cover. Bring to a boil and skim. Simmer for 20 minutes. Strain. Store in the refrigerator for up to 3 days or freeze.

Makes about 1 quart

Garnishes

Any soup or appetizer can be made to look special by adding an attractive garnish. A swirl of cream sprinkled with freshly chopped herbs such as chives and parsley, for example, is a simple but effective garnish for soups.

Croutons also complement most soups. To make them, cut day-old bread into ¼- to ½-inch cubes, or use a pastry cutter to make fancy shapes such as stars, hearts and half moons. Sauté in a little butter until crisp and golden all over. Add a clove of garlic to the butter before sautéing if desired.

Other simple ideas for soup garnishes are toasted slivered almonds, small bacon rolls on toothpicks, saffron rice and crumbled bacon.

Sprinkle julienne vegetables over soups for an elegant touch: Blanch thin strips of carrot, celery or leek in boiling salted water. Or top with fried parsley: Fry small sprigs of parsley in hot oil for a few minutes and drain well. Sprigs of fresh herbs of all kinds, lemon and lime slices, cucumber slices, onion rings and olives are other easy ideas.

HOT SOUPS

Main Meal Minestrone

2 cloves garlic,
  crushed
4 stalks celery, sliced
½ lb cabbage, sliced
2 oz spaghetti,
  broken
½ package (10 oz)
  frozen green beans
1 can (16 oz) white
  beans
4 carrots, sliced
2 onions, chopped
2 potatoes, diced
2 zucchini, sliced
⅓ cup rice
Bouquet garni
1 can (14½ oz) whole
  tomatoes
4 cups water
Salt and pepper

Place the ingredients in a deep pot. Simmer over medium heat for 30 to 40 minutes.

Remove and discard the bouquet garni. Serve hot, with hard rolls and grated Parmesan cheese.

4 servings

Mushroom Soup with Madeira

6 tablespoons butter
1 onion, finely
   chopped
1 lb mushrooms,
   finely chopped
¼ cup flour
4 cups chicken stock
   or broth
Salt and pepper
½ cup dry Madeira
⅔ cup whipping
   cream

Melt the butter in a large skillet. Add the onion and sauté for 20 minutes, or until evenly browned. Add the mushrooms and sauté for 2 minutes. Stir in the flour and cook for 1 minute.

Gradually stir in the stock and season with salt and pepper. Bring to a boil. Cover and simmer for 10 to 15 minutes.

Stir in the Madeira and cream and heat through over low heat. Serve hot, garnished with chopped parsley.

4 to 6 servings

Fennel Soup

2 tablespoons butter
1 onion, chopped
4 bulbs fennel, chopped
Bouquet garni
4 cups chicken stock or broth
Salt and pepper
3 egg yolks
Juice of 1 lemon
Fennel leaves

Melt the butter in a large skillet. Add the onion and sauté for 5 minutes, until softened. Stir in the fennel. Add the bouquet garni and stock and season with salt and pepper. Bring to a boil; reduce heat, cover and simmer for 30 minutes, until the vegetables are very tender. Beat the egg yolks and lemon juice together.

Cool the soup slightly; discard the bouquet garni. Transfer to a blender and puree until smooth. Reheat. Stir a few tablespoons of the soup into the egg yolk mixture; then stir into the warm soup.

Serve warm, garnished with fennel leaves and croutons.

6 servings

Creamy Chicken Soup

1 onion, chopped
2 stalks celery, chopped
2 carrots, chopped
1 leek, chopped
1 chicken (2½ lb)
Bouquet garni
Pinch of mace
Grated rind and juice of ½ lemon
3 tablespoons butter
6 tablespoons flour
Salt
2 egg yolks
⅔ cup whipping cream

Place the vegetables and chicken in a deep pot and add enough water to cover. Add the bouquet garni, mace, lemon rind and juice. Bring to a boil. Skim off foam; cover and simmer 1 hour, until chicken is tender.

Remove the chicken and cut off about ½ lb of meat. Dice the meat and set aside. Reserve the rest of the chicken for another dish. Strain the stock, reserving about 5 cups. Cool and skim off the fat.

Melt the butter in a large saucepan. Stir in the flour and simmer for 1 minute, without browning. Gradually stir in the reserved stock. Bring to a boil; reduce heat and simmer for 2 minutes. Add the diced chicken and season to taste with salt.

Blend the egg yolks with the cream. Remove the soup from the heat and stir in the cream mixture. Heat through and serve.

6 servings

Sun Choke Soup

2 lb Jerusalem
   artichokes
Juice of 1 lemon
2 tablespoons butter
1 onion, chopped
2½ cups chicken
   stock or broth
1¼ cups milk
⅔ cup half-and-half
2 tablespoons finely
   chopped parsley
Salt

Peel and chop the artichokes. Place in a bowl with the lemon juice and enough water to cover.

Melt the butter in a large saucepan. Add the onion and sauté until softened but not brown. Drain the artichokes and add to the pan with the stock and milk. Bring to a boil; cover and simmer for 35 to 40 minutes, until artichokes are tender.

Transfer to a blender and puree until smooth. Return to the pan and reheat. Stir in the half-and-half and parsley and season with salt.

4 to 6 servings

Tomato and Cheese Soup

2 tablespoons butter
2 onions, chopped
4 tablespoons flour
2 lb tomatoes,
  peeled, seeded and
  chopped
1 clove garlic,
  minced
Pinch each of dried
  rosemary
  and thyme
2½ cups chicken
  stock or broth
Salt and pepper
⅔ cup whipping
  cream
1 egg yolk
¼ lb Gruyère cheese,
  grated

Melt the butter in a large saucepan. Add the onions and sauté for 10 minutes, until softened but not brown. Stir in the flour and sauté 1 minute. Stir in the tomatoes, garlic, herbs and stock and season with salt and pepper.

Bring to a boil; cover and simmer for 30 minutes. Transfer to a blender and puree until smooth. Return to the saucepan.

Blend the cream with the egg yolk. Add to the pan. Warm through over a low heat; do not allow to boil or the soup will curdle.

Stir in the cheese and serve.

6 to 8 servings

Cheese and Onion Soup

3 tablespoons butter
3 onions, finely
  chopped
4 cups chicken stock
  or broth
½ cup dry white
  wine
Bouquet garni
Salt and pepper
8 slices (½ inch
  thick) French
  bread, toasted
8 slices (¼ inch
  thick) Gruyère
  cheese
3 tablespoons grated
  Parmesan cheese
½ cup grated
  Cheddar cheese

Melt the butter in a large saucepan. Add the onions and sauté for about 30 minutes, until golden brown. Add the stock, wine and bouquet garni and season with salt and pepper. Bring to a boil; cover and simmer for 20 minutes. Discard the bouquet garni.

Arrange a layer of toast in the bottom of an ovenproof tureen. Cover with a layer of the Gruyère, then sprinkle with some of the Parmesan and Cheddar. Repeat the layers once or twice, finishing with the cheeses.

Pour in the soup and bake in a 350° oven for 20 minutes, until the cheese is melted. Serve immediately.

4 to 6 servings

Puree of Chestnut Soup

1 lb chestnuts
1 tablespoon oil
¼ lb bacon, chopped
1 large onion,
    chopped
2 stalks celery,
    chopped
2 carrots, chopped
Bouquet garni
6 cups chicken stock
    or broth
Salt and pepper

Put the chestnuts in a pan of cold water, bring to a boil and simmer for 1 minute.

Hold each chestnut in a cloth and peel away the shell and inner skin with a sharp knife. If the skin does not come away, return the nut to the pan for 1 minute.

Heat the oil in a saucepan, add the bacon and onion and cook 2 minutes without browning. Add the chestnuts and remaining ingredients, except the salt and pepper, and bring to a boil. Cover and simmer for 1 hour, until the chestnuts are soft. Discard the bouquet garni and puree in a blender. Season with salt and pepper.

Serve hot, garnished with fried bacon rolls and chopped parsley.
8 servings

Cream of Corn Soup

3 tablespoons butter
1 onion, chopped
2 potatoes, diced
¼ cup flour
4 cups milk
1 bay leaf
Salt and white
    pepper
2 cans (12 oz each)
    whole kernel corn,
    drained
2 tablespoons
    whipping cream

Melt the butter in a large saucepan. Add the onion and sauté for 5 minutes, until softened but not brown. Add the potatoes and sauté 2 minutes. Stir in the flour. Gradually add the milk, stirring constantly. Bring to a boil. Add the bay leaf, season with salt and pepper and stir in half the corn. Cover and simmer for 15 to 20 minutes. Discard the bay leaf.

Transfer to a blender and puree until smooth. Return to the saucepan, add the remaining corn and heat through.

Stir in the cream and serve, sprinkled with crumbled bacon.
4 to 6 servings

Garlic Soup

2 tablespoons olive
   oil
24 cloves garlic,
   peeled
Bouquet garni
1/8 teaspoon nutmeg
1/4 teaspoon mace
4 cups beef or
   chicken stock
Salt and pepper
3 egg yolks
6 to 8 slices bread

Heat the oil in a large saucepan. Add the whole garlic cloves and sauté for 10 minutes, without browning. Add the bouquet garni, nutmeg and mace and season with salt and pepper. Stir in the stock. Bring to a boil; cover and simmer for 20 minutes.

Strain the soup and return it to the pan. Bring to a boil; remove from the heat and season with salt and pepper.

Meanwhile, blend the egg yolks with 2 tablespoons of the soup. Toast the bread on both sides and place in individual soup bowls.

Blend the egg yolk mixture into the soup, stirring constantly. Ladle over the toast in the soup bowls and serve, garnished with parsley and grated Parmesan cheese.

6 to 8 servings

Sweet Pepper Soup

3 tablespoons butter
1 onion, finely
   chopped
1 clove garlic,
   minced
1/4 cup flour
4 cups chicken stock
   or broth
1 lb sweet red
   peppers, seeded
   and chopped
1 dried red chili
   pepper, chopped
1/2 lb tomatoes,
   peeled, seeded and
   chopped
1/2 teaspoon dried
   thyme

Melt the butter in a large saucepan. Add the onion and garlic and sauté over a low heat for 2 minutes. Stir in the flour and sauté for 2 minutes. Gradually add the stock, stirring constantly. Bring to a boil. Add the red peppers, chili, tomatoes and thyme. Reduce heat, cover and simmer for 20 minutes, until the vegetables are tender.

Transfer to a blender and puree until smooth. Return the soup to the pan and heat through. Serve garnished with chopped chives.

6 servings

Eggplant and Crabmeat Soup

1 tablespoon oil
2 onions, chopped
2 cloves garlic,
  minced
4 large eggplants,
  peeled and
  chopped
1 can (14½ oz) whole
  tomatoes
1¼ cups chicken
  stock or broth
1 tablespoon tomato
  puree
Bouquet garni
½ cup dry white
  wine
Salt and pepper
1 can (6½ oz)
  crabmeat, drained

Heat the oil in a large saucepan. Add the onions and garlic and sauté over a low heat for 5 to 7 minutes, until softened but not brown. Stir in the eggplant and tomatoes with their juice. Bring to a boil slowly. Stir in the stock, tomato puree, bouquet garni and wine, and season with salt and pepper. Cover and simmer for 30 minutes, until the vegetables are very tender. Discard the bouquet garni.

Transfer to a blender and puree until smooth. Return to the pan and stir in the crabmeat. Bring to a boil.

Serve garnished with chopped parsley if desired.

6 servings

17

Saffron Seafood Chowder

2 onions, chopped
½ lb potatoes, diced
2½ cups milk
1¼ cups fish or
  chicken stock
1½ lb white fish
  fillets
4 sea scallops
½ lb shrimp, peeled
½ cup white wine
⅔ cup whipping
  cream
Pinch of saffron
Salt and pepper

Combine the onions, potatoes, milk and stock in a large saucepan and bring to a boil. Boil for 15 minutes, until vegetables are tender. Cool slightly. Transfer to a blender and puree until smooth.

Cut the fish fillets into 1½-inch pieces and coarsely chop the scallops. Return the soup to the pan and add the fish, scallops and shrimp. Simmer over a moderate heat for about 5 minutes, until cooked. Stir in the remaining ingredients, seasoning to taste with salt and pepper. Heat through.

Serve garnished with cooked shrimp.
4 to 6 servings

Mussel Chowder

2 lb mussels
½ lb white fish
  fillets, skinned
3 tablespoons butter
1 onion, chopped
2 stalks celery,
  chopped
1 clove garlic,
  minced
¼ cup flour
4 cups fish stock
⅔ cup dry white
  wine
Bouquet garni
Salt and white
  pepper
½ cup long-grain
  rice, cooked
Pinch of saffron
2 egg yolks
3 tablespoons cream

Scrub the mussels and cut the fish into 1½-inch pieces.

Melt the butter in a large saucepan. Add the onion, celery and garlic and sauté for 2 minutes, without browning. Stir in the flour and sauté for 2 minutes. Gradually stir in the stock and bring to a boil. Stir in the wine. Add the fish, mussels and bouquet garni and season with salt and pepper. Cover and simmer for 5 to 7 minutes, until the mussel shells have opened; discard any that do not.

Stir in the rice and saffron and heat through. Blend the egg yolks with the cream; then blend with a few tablespoons of the hot soup.

Remove the soup from the heat and discard the bouquet garni. Blend in the egg yolk mixture and serve, garnished with chopped parsley.
6 servings

19

Lentil Soup

1 package (1 lb)
  lentils
2 tablespoons butter
2 onions, chopped
4 leeks, chopped
4 carrots, chopped
2 stalks celery,
  chopped
8 cups beef stock or
  broth
½ cup dry sherry
Salt and pepper
½ cup diced cooked
  ham

Rinse and sort through lentils. Soak in cold water overnight and drain.

Melt the butter in a large saucepan. Add the onions and sauté until lightly browned. Stir in the leeks, carrots and celery and sauté for 2 minutes. Add the lentils, stock and sherry, and season with salt and pepper. Bring to a boil; cover and simmer for 1 hour, until the vegetables are tender.

Transfer to a blender and puree until smooth. Return to the pan and heat through. Stir in the ham and garnish with chopped parsley.

6 to 8 servings

Scotch Broth

1½ lb lamb neck
4 cups beef stock or
  broth
Bouquet garni
½ cup pearl barley
½ lb carrots, sliced
4 stalks celery,
  chopped
2 onions, sliced
2 leeks, sliced
1 turnip, diced
1 small rutabaga,
  diced
Salt and pepper
½ cup dry sherry

Trim any excess fat from the lamb and place in a deep pot with the stock and bouquet garni. Bring to a boil; skim the surface. Cover and simmer for 1½ hours, skimming the surface of the stock occasionally.

Remove the meat from the pot and set aside. Stir in the barley and the vegetables. Bring to a boil; cover and simmer for 30 minutes. Season with the salt and pepper; discard the bouquet garni.

Separate the meat from the bones and add to the pot with the sherry. Bring to a boil; reduce the heat and simmer for 5 minutes. Skim any fat from the surface before serving.

6 to 8 servings

NOTE: This soup is best made a day in advance. Refrigerate overnight. Remove solid fat from the surface. Bring to a boil, heat through and serve as a hearty main dish.

Mulligatawny Soup

1 cup lentils
2 tablespoons oil
2 onions, chopped
1 tablespoon curry
  powder
2 cloves garlic,
  minced
1 sweet red pepper,
  seeded and
  chopped
3 dried red chili
  peppers, chopped
5 cups chicken stock
  or broth
¼ cup raisins
1 can (8¼ oz) whole
  tomatoes,
  chopped
1 tablespoon tomato
  puree
Salt and pepper

Rinse and sort the lentils; drain.

Heat the oil in a large saucepan. Add the onions and sauté until browned. Stir in the curry powder and sauté 2 minutes, stirring occasionally. Add the lentils, garlic, pepper, chilies, stock, raisins, tomatoes and tomato puree. Bring to a boil. Cover and simmer for 1½ hours.

Transfer to a blender and puree until smooth. Return to the pan and season with salt and pepper.

Serve hot, with saffron rice.

8 servings

NOTE: To make saffron rice, cook rice in boiling salted water with a pinch of saffron.

Breton-Style Onion Soup

3 tablespoons butter
1 lb onions, sliced
½ lb potatoes, diced
5 cups beef stock or
  broth
Bouquet garni
Salt and pepper
Oil
4 cloves garlic, sliced
1 loaf French bread,
  sliced into ½-inch
  rounds
½ cup grated
  Cheddar cheese

Melt the butter in a large saucepan. Add the onions and sauté over low heat for 30 minutes, until golden.

Add the potatoes, stock and bouquet garni. Bring to a boil; cover and simmer for 15 to 20 minutes, until potatoes are tender. Season with salt and pepper and discard the bouquet garni.

Heat the oil and garlic in a skillet. Add the bread and sauté until golden on both sides. Drain.

Ladle the soup into individual oven-proof bowls. Float 1 or 2 slices of toast in each and sprinkle with the Cheddar. Broil under a high heat until the cheese is bubbling.

6 to 8 servings

Curried Parsnip Soup

4 tablespoons butter
1 teaspoon curry
   powder
2 large onions,
   chopped
1½ lb parsnips,
   chopped
2½ cups chicken
   stock or broth
1¼ cups milk
⅔ cup half-and-half
Salt and white
   pepper

Melt the butter in a large pan. Stir in the curry powder and sauté for 2 minutes. Add the onions and parsnips and sauté gently for 5 minutes, stirring occasionally. Add the stock and bring to a boil. Reduce the heat and simmer for 25 to 30 minutes, until the vegetables are tender.

Transfer to a blender and puree until smooth. Return to the pan and add the milk and half-and-half. Season with salt and pepper. Bring to a boil, stirring. Serve garnished with chopped apple.

6 to 8 servings

Puree of Lima Bean Soup

2 tablespoons butter
1 onion, chopped
1 stalk celery,
    chopped
¼ cup flour
4 cups chicken stock
    or broth
2 packages (10 oz
    each) frozen lima
    beans
Bouquet garni
Salt and pepper
2 egg yolks

Melt the butter in a large saucepan. Add the onion and celery and sauté for 5 minutes, without browning. Stir in the flour and sauté for 1 minute.

Gradually stir in the stock; add the beans and bouquet garni. Bring to a boil. Simmer for 35 minutes, until the beans are very tender. Season to taste with salt and pepper and discard the bouquet garni.

Transfer to a blender and puree until smooth. Blend a few tablespoons of the soup with the egg yolks in a small bowl. Return the remaining soup to the pan and heat through. Remove from the heat and let stand for 2 minutes. Blend in the egg yolks, stirring until smooth.

Serve garnished with whipped cream and chopped chives.
4 to 6 servings

Spinach and Watercress Soup

2 bunches of
  watercress
1 bunch green
  onions, chopped
½ lb spinach
1 pinch each of dried
  rosemary and
  thyme
¼ cup chopped
  parsley
2½ cups chicken
  stock or broth
Salt and pepper
1½ teaspoons
  cornstarch
½ cup whipping
  cream
Squeeze of lemon
  juice

Place the watercress, green onions and spinach in a large saucepan. Add the herbs and stock and season with salt and pepper. Bring to a boil. Reduce heat, cover and simmer for about 20 minutes.

Transfer to a blender and puree until smooth. Return to the pan and heat through.

Blend the cornstarch with the cream. Stir into the soup and simmer gently, stirring constantly, until thickened. Stir in the lemon juice.

Serve garnished with lemon slices.

4 to 6 servings

Bean Soup with Pistou

¾ cup navy beans
¼ cup kidney beans
2 onions
2 stalks celery
2 carrots
¼ lb zucchini
2 tablespoons butter
2 cloves garlic,
    minced
1 can (14½ oz) whole
    tomatoes
½ cup dry red wine
1½ cups beef stock
    or broth
Bouquet garni
1 tablespoon
    Worcestershire
    sauce
1 tablespoon tomato
    puree
Salt and pepper
PISTOU:
4 cloves garlic
1 bunch basil
¼ cup olive oil
¼ cup pine nuts

Soak the beans separately in cold water overnight. Rinse and drain. Place in a large saucepan with enough cold water to cover, bring to a boil and boil steadily for 10 minutes. Reduce heat, cover and simmer for 1¼ hours, until the beans are tender. Drain and set aside.

Chop the onions, celery and carrots and slice the zucchini. Melt the butter in a large saucepan. Add the onions and sauté until golden. Add the garlic, celery, carrots, tomatoes with their juice, wine, stock and bouquet garni. Bring to a boil; reduce heat, cover and simmer for 20 minutes. Stir in the zucchini, Worcestershire and tomato puree. Simmer 5 minutes; then add the beans and season with salt and pepper. Heat through.

To make the pistou, combine the garlic, basil, oil and pine nuts in a blender and puree until smooth. Blend into the soup before serving. Serve with grated Parmesan cheese.
6 to 8 servings

Cream of Zucchini Soup

2 tablespoons butter
2 onions, chopped
1½ lb zucchini,
    chopped
4 cups beef stock or
    broth
2 tablespoons dry
    sherry
Bouquet garni
Salt and pepper
⅔ cup whipping
    cream

Melt the butter in a large saucepan. Add the onions and sauté gently for 5 minutes. Stir in the zucchini and sauté gently for 10 minutes.

Add the stock, sherry and bouquet garni. Bring to a boil; reduce heat, cover and simmer for 30 minutes. Discard the bouquet garni.

Transfer the soup to a blender and puree until smooth. Return to the pan and season with salt and pepper. Stir in the cream and heat through.

Serve garnished with croutons.
6 servings

COLD SOUPS

Cucumber and Yogurt Soup

1 cucumber, peeled
 and chopped
1¼ cups plain yogurt
1¼ cups milk
1 clove garlic
10 mint leaves
Salt and pepper

Place the cucumber, yogurt, milk, garlic and mint in a blender and puree until smooth. Season with salt and pepper. Refrigerate until chilled.

Pour into a chilled tureen or individual iced soup bowls and serve, garnished with mint leaves.

6 servings

Gazpacho

1 lb ripe tomatoes
1 onion
2 cloves garlic
1 cucumber
1 green pepper
3 tablespoons olive oil
2 tablespoons wine vinegar
1¼ cups tomato juice
Salt and pepper
1¼ cups water

Peel and chop the tomatoes, onion, garlic and half the cucumber and place in a blender. Dice the remaining cucumber and the green pepper and reserve.

Add the oil, vinegar and tomato juice to the blender and puree until smooth. Pour into a tureen, stir in the water, season with salt and pepper and chill.

Serve with bowls of the reserved cucumber, green pepper and croutons. Garnish with green pepper if desired.
6 servings

Cream of Carrot Soup

2 tablespoons butter
1 lb carrots, sliced
1 onion, chopped
4 cups chicken stock
   or broth
Pinch of sugar
Grated rind of
   1 orange
Juice of 4 oranges
Salt and pepper
⅔ cup half-and-half

Melt the butter in a large saucepan. Add the carrots and onion and sauté for 10 minutes, without browning.

Stir in the stock and sugar. Bring to a boil; cover and simmer for 1 hour.

Transfer to a blender and puree until smooth. Pour into a tureen and stir in the orange rind and juice. Season with salt and pepper. Chill for several hours.

Stir in the cream just before serving.
6 servings

Vichyssoise

4 tablespoons butter
2 onions, chopped
4 leeks, white part only, chopped
4 potatoes, diced
5 cups chicken stock or broth
Bouquet garni
Salt and white pepper
⅔ cup whipping cream

Melt the butter in a large saucepan. Add the onions and sauté for 10 minutes, without browning.

Stir in the leeks, potatoes, stock and bouquet garni. Bring to a boil; cover and simmer for 30 to 40 minutes, stirring occasionally. Discard the bouquet garni.

Transfer the soup to a blender and puree until smooth. Season with salt and pepper. Let cool, then chill for 3 to 4 hours.

Stir in the cream just before serving. Garnish with chopped chives and croutons.

6 servings

NOTE: This soup can also be served hot with leftover cooked vegetables. Puree the vegetables if desired.

Minted Cucumber Soup

1 tablespoon oil
1 onion, chopped
2 cucumbers, peeled
  and diced
1 potato, chopped
4 cups chicken stock
  or broth
Bouquet garni
Salt and white
  pepper
⅔ cup half-and-half
2 tablespoons finely
  chopped mint

Heat the oil in a large saucepan. Add the onion and sauté until softened. Stir in the cucumber, potato, stock and bouquet garni. Bring to a boil; cover and simmer for 20 to 25 minutes. Discard the bouquet garni.

Transfer to a blender and puree until smooth. Season with salt and pepper. Stir in the cream and chopped mint and chill for 2 to 3 hours before serving.

Serve cold, garnished with mint sprigs.

4 to 6 servings

Iced Tomato and Basil Soup

2 lb ripe tomatoes
1 tablespoon oil
1 onion, chopped
1 clove garlic,
  minced
¼ cup flour
1 tablespoon
  Worcestershire
  sauce
2 drops hot pepper
  sauce
1 cup dry white wine
1 tablespoon tomato
  puree
Salt and pepper
3 tablespoons
  chopped basil

Coarsely chop the tomatoes. Heat the oil in a large saucepan. Add the onion and garlic and sauté for 5 minutes without browning. Stir in the flour and cook, stirring, for 2 minutes.

Stir in the chopped tomatoes. Cover and simmer gently for about 20 minutes, stirring occasionally.

Stir in the Worcestershire and hot pepper sauce, wine and tomato puree. Bring to a boil; cover and simmer for 30 minutes.

Transfer to a blender and puree until smooth. Season to taste with salt and pepper. Strain into a bowl. Let cool, then stir in the chopped basil; chill for several hours.

Serve the soup well chilled in chilled soup bowls. If desired, garnish with a swirl of whipped cream and a sprinkling of chopped chives.

6 servings

Iced Avocado Soup

2 ripe avocados
Juice of ½ lemon
4 cups chicken stock or broth
⅔ cup whipping cream
2 drops hot pepper sauce
Cayenne pepper
Salt

Cut the avocados in half and remove the pits. Scoop out the flesh and puree with the lemon juice in a blender.

Transfer to a mixing bowl, stir in the stock and cream and season with the pepper sauce and a pinch of cayenne and salt. Chill for several hours.

Serve garnished with lemon slices and parsley sprigs.

4 to 6 servings

Chilled Shrimp Bisque

2 tablespoons butter
1 onion, chopped
1 clove garlic, minced
¼ cup flour
1 can (14½ oz) plus 1 can (8¼ oz) whole tomatoes
Juice of ½ lemon
Bouquet garni
Salt and pepper
2 tablespoons dry white wine
½ lb cod or haddock fillets, cut into 1-inch pieces
¾ lb shrimp, peeled and coarsely chopped

Melt the butter in a large saucepan. Add the onion and garlic and sauté for 5 minutes, without browning.

Stir in the flour and sauté for 2 minutes. Gradually stir in the tomatoes and their juice and the lemon juice. Add the bouquet garni. Bring to a boil. Cover and simmer for 25 minutes. Discard the bouquet garni.

Transfer to a blender and puree until smooth. Return to the pan and season with salt and pepper. Stir in the wine, fish and shrimp. Simmer for 5 to 7 minutes, until the fish is tender.

Pour into a tureen and chill for several hours before serving.

6 servings

Chilled Almond Soup

1 tablespoon butter
1 onion, chopped
¼ cup flour
4 cups chicken stock
   or broth
1½ cups slivered
   almonds
1 bay leaf
Salt
⅔ cup whipping
   cream

Melt the butter in a large saucepan. Add the onion and sauté for 5 minutes, until softened.

Stir in the flour and sauté for 1 minute, without browning. Gradually stir in the stock, stirring constantly. Add the almonds and bay leaf. Bring to a boil. Cover and simmer for 20 minutes. Discard the bay leaf.

Transfer to a blender and puree until smooth. Season with salt. Pour into a bowl and chill for 2 to 3 hours.

Just before serving, stir in the cream. Garnish with a sprinkle of toasted almonds.

4 to 6 servings

Chilled Watercress Soup

2 bunches
  watercress
2 tablespoons butter
2 leeks, thinly sliced
1 onion, chopped
½ lb potatoes, diced
2½ cups chicken
  stock or broth
Salt and pepper
1¼ cups milk

Remove the stems from the watercress and coarsely chop the leaves.

Melt the butter in a large saucepan. Add the leeks and onion and sauté for 5 minutes, without browning. Add the potatoes and sauté 2 minutes. Add the watercress and the stock, and season with salt and pepper. Bring to a boil. Cover and simmer for 25 minutes.

Transfer to a blender and puree until smooth. Pour into a bowl and stir in the milk. Chill for several hours.

Serve garnished with croutons.

4 to 6 servings

Summer Vegetable Soup

8 large tomatoes
2 cloves garlic
½ onion
½ cucumber
1 green pepper,
  seeded
1 red pepper, seeded
Pinch each thyme
  and basil
2 sprigs parsley
Salt
6 tablespoons olive
  oil
¼ cup lemon juice
2½ cups chilled
  tomato juice
Few drops hot
  pepper sauce

Coarsely chop the tomatoes, garlic, onion, cucumber and green and red peppers. Process in a blender until smooth. Add the thyme, basil and parsley and season with salt; mix well. Chill for several hours.

Combine the olive oil, lemon juice, tomato juice and hot pepper sauce. Strain the soup into a bowl. Gradually stir in the oil and tomato juice mixture just before serving. Serve garnished with croutons.

6 servings

SALADS

Mushroom and Bean Sprout Salad

¾ lb button
   mushrooms
1 red pepper, seeded
⅓ cup Vinaigrette
   Dressing (page 64)
½ lb bean sprouts

Cut the mushrooms in quarters. Slice the red pepper.

Combine the mushrooms and the vinaigrette in a salad bowl and toss. Let marinate for 1 hour, tossing occasionally. Add the bean sprouts and pepper and toss again. Garnish with lemon slices and parsley if desired.

6 servings

Cauliflower Salad

1 small cauliflower
Salt
1 bunch watercress
4 green onions,
  chopped
5 tablespoons
  French Dressing
  (page 63)
1 tablespoon sesame
  seeds, toasted

Break the cauliflower into flowerets.
Boil in salted water for 3 minutes.
Drain and cool.

  Add the watercress, green onions
and dressing and toss thoroughly.
Transfer to a salad bowl and sprinkle
with the sesame seeds.
6 servings

Chinese Cabbage Salad

1 small head
  Chinese cabbage
1 bunch watercress
4 oranges,
  segmented
1/3 cup Mint and
  Honey Dressing
  (page 64)

Shred the cabbage and place in a salad bowl with the watercress and orange segments. Add the dressing and toss thoroughly.
6 servings

Celery and Apple Salad

1 bunch celery,
  thinly sliced
4 red apples, thinly
  sliced
4 tablespoons
  Vinaigrette
  Dressing (page 64)
1 tablespoon sesame
  seeds, toasted

Combine the sliced celery and apples in a salad bowl. Add the dressing and toss well. Add the sesame seeds and toss again.
6 servings

Lima Bean Salad

2 packages (10 oz
  each) frozen lima
  beans
Juice of 1/2 lemon
1 teaspoon oil
3 tablespoons plain
  yogurt
4 tablespoons
  Mayonnaise
  (page 62)
2 teaspoons chopped
  mixed herbs
  (parsley, thyme,
  chives)

Cook the beans following package directions. Drain and place in a bowl. Mix in the lemon juice and oil and let cool.

Combine the yogurt, mayonnaise and herbs. Pour the dressing over the beans and mix well. Transfer to a salad bowl. Garnish with additional herbs.
4 to 6 servings

Swedish Potato Salad

1½ lb small new
  potatoes
Salt
2 tablespoons
  French Dressing
  (page 63)
1 beet, cooked and
  diced
1 dill pickle, diced
5 tablespoons
  Yogurt Dressing
  (page 62)

Scrub the potatoes well, leaving the skins on. Boil in salted water until fork tender, 20 to 35 minutes depending on their size. Drain, dice and toss with the French dressing while still warm. Let cool.

Add the beet, pickle and yogurt dressing and toss well. Transfer to a salad bowl. Serve sprinkled with chopped dill.
6 servings

Potato and Radish Vinaigrette

1 lb small new
  potatoes
Salt
¼ cup Vinaigrette
  Dressing (page 64)
4 green onions,
  sliced
1 bunch radishes,
  thinly sliced

Scrub the potatoes well, leaving the skins on. Boil in salted water until fork tender, about 20 to 35 minutes. Drain, dice and toss with the dressing while still warm. Let cool.

Add the green onions and radishes and toss well. Transfer to a salad bowl.
4 servings

Mixed Bean Salad

1 package (10 oz)
  frozen lima beans
1 package (10 oz)
  frozen cut green
  beans
1 can (16 oz) kidney
  beans
1 can (16 oz) white
  beans
6 green onions,
  chopped
1 cup French
  Dressing (page 63)
2 tablespoons
  chopped parsley

Cook the lima beans and green beans according to package directions. Combine all the beans in a bowl, add the green onions and toss with the dressing while still warm. Let cool.

Add the parsley and toss. Transfer to a salad bowl.
12 servings

Coleslaw with Yogurt Dressing

½ medium head
  cabbage
2 red apples
2 stalks celery
1 onion
½ cup raisins
½ cup chopped
  walnuts
2 tablespoons
  chopped parsley
½ cup Yogurt
  Dressing (page 62)

Finely shred the cabbage. Chop the apples. Finely chop the celery and onion.

Combine the ingredients in a bowl and toss thoroughly. Transfer to a salad bowl to serve.

6 servings

Brown Rice Salad

½ lb brown rice
Salt
3 green onions,
   finely chopped
1 red pepper, seeded
   and chopped
½ cup raisins
½ cup chopped
   toasted cashew
   nuts
2 tablespoons
   chopped parsley
⅓ cup Soy Sauce
   Dressing (page 64)

Boil the rice according to package
directions, about 40 to 45 minutes.
Cool. Combine the rice and the remaining ingredients in a bowl. Toss
thoroughly and serve.
6 servings

Lentil and Tomato Salad

1 cup lentils
Salt and pepper
⅓ cup Tomato and
    Garlic Dressing
    (page 62)
4 green onions,
    chopped
4 tomatoes, peeled
    and chopped
2 stalks celery, sliced
1 tablespoon
    chopped parsley

Rinse and sort through the lentils. Place in a saucepan with enough cold salted water to cover and simmer gently for 30 to 40 minutes, until softened. Drain and mix with the dressing while still warm. Let cool.

Add the remaining ingredients and season with salt and pepper. Toss well. Transfer to a salad bowl and serve.
6 servings

Spinach and Mushroom Salad

½ lb button
    mushrooms,
    sliced
4 tablespoons
    French Dressing
    (page 63)
½ lb spinach
4 green onions,
    chopped

Toss the mushrooms with 3 tablespoons of the dressing in a mixing bowl and let marinate for 1 hour, tossing occasionally.

Meanwhile, wash and thoroughly dry the spinach leaves. Remove the thick center stems and tear the leaves into a salad bowl. Add the marinated mushrooms, green onions and remaining dressing. Toss well and serve.
4 servings

Lima Bean and Cauliflower Salad

1 head cauliflower,
    broken into
    flowerets
1 package (10 oz)
    frozen lima beans,
    cooked
¼ lb button
    mushrooms,
    sliced
⅓ cup Green Herb
    Dressing (page 63)

Boil the cauliflower for 3 minutes. Drain and cool.

Combine the beans, cauliflower and mushrooms in a salad bowl. Add the dressing, toss thoroughly and serve.
6 to 8 servings

Zucchini à la Grecque

1¼ cups dry white
  wine
Juice of 2 lemons
⅔ cup water
5 tablespoons olive
  oil
1 sprig thyme
  (optional)
1 sprig parsley
1 bay leaf
½ teaspoon ground
  coriander
Salt and pepper
1 lb zucchini,
  thickly sliced

Combine the wine, lemon juice, water, oil and herbs and coriander in a saucepan and season with salt and pepper. Bring to a boil. Add the sliced zucchini, bring the liquid back to a boil and boil rapidly for 1 minute. Lift the zucchini out of the liquid with a slotted spoon, drain and set aside. Simmer the cooking liquid over moderate heat until it is well reduced. Remove from the heat and let cool.

Place the zucchini in a serving dish, add the reduced cooking liquid and chill. Serve cold, sprinkled with a bit of chopped fennel.

4 servings

Ratatouille

1 eggplant, sliced
Salt and pepper
¼ cup olive oil
2 onions, sliced
3 zucchini, sliced
4 tomatoes, peeled
  and sliced
1 clove garlic,
  minced
1 bay leaf

Place the eggplant slices in a colander, sprinkle liberally with salt and let stand for 30 minutes. Rinse, drain and pat dry with paper towels.

Heat the oil in a large skillet. Add the onions and sauté until softened. Add the eggplant, zucchini, tomatoes, garlic and bay leaf and season with salt and pepper. Stir well. Cover and simmer for about 30 minutes, until the vegetables are tender. Transfer to a serving dish and serve warm, or refrigerate for several hours and serve cold.

4 servings

NOTE: Ratatouille may also be frozen, and is an excellent dish to have on hand. To reheat, turn into a saucepan and thaw over low heat, stirring occasionally. Bring to a boil and simmer for 5 minutes.

Watercress and Egg Salad

6 slices white bread
Olive oil
2 bunches
 watercress
4 hard-cooked eggs
4 green onions
1 green pepper,
 seeded
Salt and pepper
DRESSING:
⅓ cup crumbled
 blue cheese
2 tablespoons each
 mayonnaise and
 whipping cream
1 tablespoon each
 chopped parsley
 and chives
Pinch of cayenne
 pepper

Remove the crusts and cut the bread into small cubes. Heat about ⅛ inch of oil in a large skillet, add the bread cubes and sauté until golden brown on all sides. Drain on paper towels.

Break the watercress into sprigs and place in a large salad bowl. Chop the eggs, green onions and green pepper. Add to the bowl and season with salt and pepper.

Beat the cheese with the mayonnaise and cream until very smooth. Add the herbs and cayenne and season with salt to taste.

Spoon the dressing over the salad. Add the croutons and toss well.

4 servings

Piquant Winter Salad

1 lb new potatoes
1 onion
2 stalks celery
2 carrots, grated
2 Belgian endives
¼ lb ham
4 to 5 slices salami
Salt and pepper
DRESSING:
3 hard-cooked eggs
⅔ cup sour cream
2 tablespoons
 mayonnaise
2 tablespoons
 chopped chives
1 teaspoon prepared
 mustard
2 tablespoons green
 peppercorns
1 tablespoon
 chopped parsley

Boil the potatoes in their skins in salted water for 15 to 20 minutes, until tender. Drain. Peel, slice and place in a salad bowl.

Chop the onion and celery and add to the salad bowl with the carrots. Reserve a few endive leaves for garnish. Slice the remaining endive and the ham. Dice the salami. Add to the salad bowl and season with salt and pepper. Toss well.

Cut the eggs in half and separate the whites from the yolks. Chop the whites and press the yolks through a sieve. Blend the sour cream, mayonnaise, chives, mustard, peppercorns and parsley. Add the chopped egg whites and season with salt and pepper. Spoon over the salad and toss.

Garnish with the reserved endive and sprinkle with the sieved egg yolks.

4 servings

Saffron Rice and Nut Salad

2 cloves garlic
5 tablespoons olive oil
2 onions, chopped
1 cup long-grain rice
Few strands saffron
2 cups chicken stock or broth
Salt and pepper
1 teaspoon Dijon mustard
1 teaspoon honey
2 tablespoons lemon or lime juice
1 tablespoon each chopped parsley and chives
1 cup raisins
¼ lb lean bacon
½ cup each salted peanuts and cashews

Mince 1 garlic clove and set aside. Slice the other clove. Heat 1 tablespoon of the oil in a large skillet. Add the sliced garlic and the onions and sauté until lightly browned. Stir in the rice, saffron and stock. Season with salt. Bring to a boil; cover and simmer for 12 minutes.

Meanwhile, combine the minced garlic, mustard, honey, remaining oil, and lemon juice in a salad bowl. Season with salt and pepper. Stir in the parsley, chives and raisins. Cook the bacon until crisp; crumble.

Drain the rice and let cool slightly. Add to the salad bowl along with the peanuts and cashews and mix thoroughly with the dressing. Sprinkle the bacon over the rice. Garnish with lemon.

4 servings

Pepper and Salami Salad

2 each green, red and
yellow peppers
6 tomatoes
4 hard-cooked eggs
8 slices salami
2 cans (2 oz each)
anchovy fillets,
drained
24 black olives
DRESSING:
2 cloves garlic,
minced
1 tablespoon each
chopped parsley,
chives, tarragon
and chervil
1 teaspoon grainy
mustard
1 teaspoon honey
3 tablespoons lemon
juice
⅓ cup olive oil
Salt and pepper

Roast the whole peppers under a hot
broiler until the skins are charred.
Cool. Rinse away the charred skin
under running water, seed and cut into
rings.

Slice the tomatoes and eggs into
thick rounds and arrange in the bottom of a salad bowl. Chop the salami
and sprinkle into the bowl. Place the
peppers around the edge.

Arrange the anchovy fillets in a lat-
tice pattern over the salad and place
the olives on top.

Combine the garlic, herbs, mustard,
honey, lemon juice and olive oil in a
bowl and season with salt and pepper.
Blend well and spoon over the salad.

Chill for 20 minutes before serving.
4 servings

Sausage and Cheese Salad

½ lb cabbage,
    shredded
2 carrots, grated
1 stalk celery,
    chopped
1 Belgian endive,
    shredded
¼ lb smoked cheese,
    cubed
¼ lb cooked sausage,
    peeled and cubed
DRESSING:
3 tablespoons
    mayonnaise
3 tablespoons plain
    yogurt
½ teaspoon caraway
    seeds, crushed
Salt and pepper

Combine the cabbage, carrots, celery, endive, cheese and sausage in a salad bowl.

Blend together the mayonnaise, yogurt and caraway seeds and season with salt and pepper.

Pour the dressing over the salad and toss thoroughly.

4 servings

Cheddar Log with Salad

4 hard-cooked eggs,
    chopped
½ lb sharp Cheddar
    cheese, grated
1 clove garlic,
    minced
2 tablespoons
    mayonnaise
2 tablespoons
    half-and-half
1 tablespoon
    chopped parsley
Salt and pepper
1 small head lettuce
½ cucumber, sliced
½ green pepper,
    seeded and sliced
4 tomatoes, sliced

Combine the eggs, cheese, garlic, mayonnaise, half-and-half and parsley in a bowl. Season with salt and pepper and mix well. With wet hands, shape the mixture into a log about 2 inches in diameter. Wrap in foil and chill for at least 1 hour.

Wash and dry the lettuce leaves thoroughly and arrange on an oval serving platter. Arrange the cucumber, green pepper and tomatoes at either end of the platter. Remove the foil and slice the cheese log into 8 pieces. Place in the middle of the platter between the sliced vegetables.

4 servings

Kidney Bean and Artichoke Salad

1 can (16 oz) kidney
  beans
1 can (16 oz)
  cannellini beans
1 can (14 oz)
  artichoke hearts
1 green pepper
4 green onions
2 stalks celery
2 hard-cooked eggs
1 clove garlic,
  minced
½ cup Mayonnaise
  (page 62)
1 tablespoon each
  chopped parsley,
  basil and thyme
Lemon juice
Salt and pepper
1 tablespoon capers
¼ lb lean bacon

Turn the beans into a colander, rinse under cold water and allow to drain thoroughly. Drain and quarter the artichokes. Place the drained beans and artichokes in a salad bowl.

Seed the pepper and chop, along with the green onions and celery. Add to the salad bowl. Quarter the eggs and arrange around the edge of the bowl, reserving some for garnish if desired.

Blend the garlic, mayonnaise, herbs and a squeeze of lemon juice together. Season with salt and pepper. Add the capers. Spoon over the salad and toss well.

Cook the bacon until crisp. Crumble and sprinkle over the salad. Garnish with reserved egg.

4 servings

Bean Salad with Salami

1 can (16 oz) each
  kidney beans,
  chick peas and
  white beans
1 cup French
  Dressing (page 63)
½ cup chopped
  mixed herbs
1 onion, chopped
¼ lb sliced salami,
  slivered
Salt and pepper

Rinse the beans under cold water.
Drain thoroughly and mix together in
a salad bowl. Add the French dressing
and mix well.

Add the remaining ingredients, seasoning with the salt and pepper.
12 servings

Lima Bean Vinaigrette

½ lb dried lima
   beans, soaked
   overnight
Salt
¼ cup Vinaigrette
   Dressing (page 64)
4 green onions,
   chopped
1 clove garlic,
   minced
1 tablespoon
   chopped parsley

Drain and rinse the beans and place in a
saucepan with enough cold water to
cover. Bring to a boil; cover and simmer gently for 1 to 1¼ hours, adding a
little salt near the end of cooking.

Drain the beans thoroughly, place in
a bowl and toss, while still warm, with
the vinaigrette. Add the onions and
garlic and mix well. Allow to cool.

Sprinkle with the parsley and serve.
4 servings

Melon, Tomato and Grape Salad

2 small honeydew
   melons
4 tomatoes,
   quartered
½ lb black grapes,
   seeded
¼ cup Mint and
   Honey Dressing
   (page 64)
1 tablespoon sesame
   seeds, toasted

Cut the melons in half and discard the seeds. Scoop out the flesh with a melon baller, or cut into cubes; reserve the shells.

Combine the melon, tomatoes and grapes in a mixing bowl. Add the dressing and toss well. Spoon into the melon shells. Sprinkle with the sesame seeds and garnish with mint.
4 servings

59

Pears and Blue Cheese

½ cup crumbled
  blue cheese
⅔ cup plain yogurt
2 pears, peeled,
  halved and cored
½ cup small-curd
  cottage cheese
Salt and pepper
Shredded lettuce

Mash the blue cheese with 1 tablespoon of the yogurt. Spoon into the
cavity of each pear half.

Beat the remaining yogurt with the
cottage cheese in a small bowl. Season
with salt and pepper.

Arrange the shredded lettuce on a
serving dish and place the pears, cut
sides down, on top. Spoon the yogurt
and cottage cheese mixture over the
top and chill.

Serve cold, garnished with chopped
chives.

4 servings

Hot Fruit Salad

1½ cups dried apricots
1 cup each dried prunes, dried figs and dried apples
2½ cups apple juice
2 tablespoons Calvados or brandy
¼ cup coarsely chopped walnuts

Combine the dried fruits in a mixing bowl with the apple juice and let soak overnight.

Transfer to a large saucepan and simmer for 10 to 15 minutes. Turn into a glass serving bowl and stir in the Calvados. Sprinkle with the walnuts and serve warm. Accompany with yogurt if desired.

6 servings

NOTE: If desired, this fruit salad can be made ahead of time and served as a cold dish.

Mayonnaise

1 egg yolk
¼ teaspoon each
    salt, pepper and
    dry mustard
⅔ cup olive oil
1 to 2 teaspoons
    cider vinegar

Beat the egg yolk with the seasonings until thick and pale. Add ⅓ cup of the oil, drop by drop, beating constantly, until thickened. Add the remaining oil in a slow, steady stream, beating constantly. Stir in the vinegar.
Makes about ⅔ cup

Tomato and Garlic Dressing

1¼ cups tomato
    juice
1 tablespoon lemon
    juice
2 tablespoons
    chopped chives
1 clove garlic, minced
2 tablespoons oil

Place the tomato juice, lemon juice, chives, garlic and oil in a screw-top jar. Season with salt and pepper, if desired, and shake well.
Makes about 1¼ cups

Yogurt Dressing

1¼ cups plain yogurt
2 tablespoons lemon
    juice
1 clove garlic,
    minced
Salt and pepper

Place all ingredients in a mixing bowl and season with ½ teaspoon each salt and pepper. Beat together thoroughly. Store in an airtight container in the refrigerator.
Makes about 1¼ cups

French Dressing

¾ cup olive oil
¼ cup wine vinegar
1 teaspoon Dijon
  mustard
1 clove garlic,
  minced
Salt and pepper

Place the oil, vinegar, mustard and garlic in a screw-top jar. Season with salt and pepper and shake well.
Makes about 1 cup

Green Herb Dressing

½ cup parsley sprigs
¼ cup mint leaves
¼ cup chopped
  chives
1 clove garlic,
  chopped
1 cup plain yogurt
½ cup oil
Juice of ½ lemon
Salt and pepper

Place the herbs in a blender with the garlic, yogurt, oil and lemon juice and season with salt and pepper. Puree until smooth.
Makes about 1½ cups

Mint and Honey Dressing

2 tablespoons honey
4 tablespoons cider
  vinegar
3 tablespoons olive
  oil
1 tablespoon
  chopped mint
Salt and pepper

Place the honey, vinegar, oil and mint in a screw-top jar or small mixing bowl. Season with salt and pepper and shake or whisk together well.
Makes about ⅔ cup

Vinaigrette Dressing

¾ cup olive oil
2 tablespoons cider
  vinegar
2 tablespoons lemon
  juice
1 clove garlic,
  minced
½ teaspoon prepared
  mustard
2 tablespoons
  chopped mixed
  herbs (parsley,
  chives and basil)
Salt and pepper

Place the oil, vinegar, lemon juice, garlic, mustard and herbs in a screw-top jar or small mixing bowl. Season with salt and pepper and shake or whisk together thoroughly.
Makes about 1 cup

Soy Sauce Dressing

¾ cup olive oil
¼ cup soy sauce
2 tablespoons lemon
  juice
1 clove garlic,
  minced
½-inch piece
  gingerroot, finely
  chopped
Salt and pepper

Place the oil, soy sauce, lemon juice, garlic and chopped gingerroot in a screw-top jar or small mixing bowl. Season with the salt and pepper and shake or whisk together thoroughly.
Makes about 1¼ cups

SNACKS & SUPPERS

Eggs with Vegetable Hash

2 tablespoons olive oil
1 onion, chopped
2 red peppers, seeded and cut in strips
6 slices bacon, chopped
2 boiled potatoes, diced
1 cup shelled fresh or frozen peas
4 tomatoes, chopped
1 tablespoon chopped parsley
Salt and pepper
4 eggs

Heat the oil in a 10-inch skillet. Add the onion, peppers and bacon and sauté for 5 to 6 minutes. Add the potatoes and sauté until lightly browned. Stir in the peas, tomatoes and parsley; season with salt and pepper. Sauté over low heat for 10 minutes, adding water, if necessary, to keep the mixture from sticking.

Transfer to 2 or 4 greased oven-proof dishes. Make hollows in the mixture and break an egg into each one. Bake in a 350° oven for 15 minutes, until the egg whites are just set. Serve hot.

4 servings

Spinach Omelet

3 tablespoons butter
½ lb spinach,
   shredded
1 tablespoon plain
   yogurt
Grated nutmeg
Salt and pepper
4 eggs

Melt 2 tablespoons of the butter in a small saucepan. Add the spinach and sauté over a moderate heat for 4 to 5 minutes, stirring occasionally. Remove from the heat and stir in the yogurt. Season with nutmeg, salt and pepper and keep warm.

Beat the eggs in a bowl and season with salt and pepper. Melt the remaining butter in a 10-inch omelet pan until foaming. Add the eggs and cook over high heat until the omelet begins to set. Lift the edge and tilt the pan to let the unset egg run underneath. Spread the filling over half the omelet. Carefully fold the omelet in half.

Slide onto a warm plate and serve.

2 servings

Shrimp Omelet

5 oz frozen baby
   shrimp, thawed
3 tablespoons dry
   white wine
1 small bay leaf
1 sprig parsley
3 tablespoons
   whipping cream
Salt and pepper
2 tablespoons butter
3 eggs, lightly beaten

Combine the shrimp, wine, bay leaf and parsley in a small saucepan and simmer, uncovered, over moderate heat until all the excess liquid has evaporated. Discard the bay leaf and parsley and stir in the cream. Season with salt and pepper.

Melt the butter in an 8-inch omelet pan until foaming. Add the eggs and cook over high heat until just beginning to set. Gently lift the edge and tilt the pan to let the unset egg run underneath. Spread the filling over half the omelet. Fold over the other half.

Slide onto a warm plate and serve, garnished with shrimp.

1 or 2 servings

Smoked Whitefish Omelet

4 tablespoons butter
4 tablespoons
   half-and-half
¼ lb smoked
   whitefish, flaked
Salt and pepper
3 eggs, separated
2 tablespoons grated
   Parmesan cheese

Melt 2 tablespoons of the butter in a small saucepan. Remove from the heat and stir in 2 tablespoons of the half-and-half and the fish. Season with salt and pepper. Stir in the egg yolks.

Whip the egg whites until just stiff enough to form peaks. Gently fold in the fish mixture and 1 tablespoon of the cheese.

Melt the remaining butter in an 8-inch omelet pan. Pour in the omelet mixture and spread evenly in the pan. Cook over moderate heat until just beginning to set.

Sprinkle with the remaining cheese, transfer to the broiler and broil until lightly browned. Slide the unfolded omelet onto a warmed plate. Pour the remaining cream over the top and serve, garnished with parsley.

2 servings

Spanish Omelet

6 tablespoons butter
1 onion, chopped
1 each small red and
　green pepper,
　seeded and cut
　into strips
1 potato, diced
1 carrot, diced
1 zucchini, sliced
1 to 2 cloves garlic,
　minced
Salt and pepper
4 eggs, lightly beaten

Melt 4 tablespoons of the butter in a 10-inch skillet. Add the onion, peppers, potato, carrot, zucchini and garlic, cover and simmer for 10 minutes, until tender, shaking the skillet frequently. Season with salt and pepper.

Melt the remaining butter in a 10-inch omelet pan until foaming. Add the cooked vegetables and their liquid. Pour in the eggs and shake the pan gently to distribute the ingredients evenly. Cook over low heat until the omelet is set.

Slide the unfolded omelet onto a warmed plate and serve hot.

2 servings

Ham Soufflé Omelet

2 tablespoons oil
1 small onion,
   chopped
½ cup sliced
   mushrooms
¼ cup shredded ham
1 tablespoon
   chopped parsley
2 tablespoons
   whipping cream
Salt and pepper
4 eggs, separated
2 tablespoons milk

Heat 1 tablespoon of the oil in a small skillet. Add the onion and sauté until softened. Add the mushrooms and sauté for 1 minute. Stir in the ham, parsley and cream, and season with salt and pepper. Keep warm.

Beat the egg yolks with the milk in a small bowl and season with salt and pepper. Beat the egg whites until stiff; fold into the yolk mixture.

Heat the remaining oil in a 9-inch omelet pan. Pour in the soufflé mixture and spread evenly over the pan. Cook over moderate heat for 1 minute, until golden brown underneath.

Transfer the pan to a 400° oven for 3 minutes, or until the top is set.

Loosen the omelet from the edges of the pan. Spread the warm filling over one half of the omelet and gently fold the omelet in half. Transfer to a warmed plate and serve.

2 servings

70

Herbed Cheese Soufflé

2 tablespoons butter
¼ cup flour
⅔ cup milk
3 eggs, separated, plus 1 egg white
½ cup grated Gruyère cheese
¼ cup grated Cheddar cheese
1 tablespoon chopped chives
1 tablespoon chopped parsley
Salt
Cayenne pepper

Melt the butter in a small saucepan over moderate heat. Blend in the flour and cook for 1 minute. Stir in the milk and bring to a boil, stirring constantly. Reduce heat and simmer for 1 minute. Cool slightly.

Whisk the egg yolks lightly with the cheeses, chives and parsley, and season with salt and cayenne. Blend a tablespoon of the milk mixture into the egg yolks, then stir the yolks into the milk mixture.

Beat the egg whites until stiff. Fold 1 tablespoon into the milk mixture. Gently fold in the remaining whites.

Turn into a greased 5-cup soufflé dish and bake in a 375° oven for 25 to 30 minutes.

Garnish with paprika and chopped chives and serve immediately.

4 servings

Creamed Mushrooms on Toast

4 tablespoons butter
1 onion, chopped
¾ lb button
  mushrooms
2 tablespoons flour
1¼ cups milk
Dash of
  Worcestershire
  sauce
2 tablespoons
  half-and-half
Salt and pepper
Juice of ½ lemon
4 slices hot buttered
  toast

Melt the butter in a skillet. Add the onion and sauté for 5 to 7 minutes, without browning, until softened. Add the mushrooms and sauté for 1 minute, stirring. Sprinkle the flour over and mix well. Gradually add the milk, stirring constantly. Bring to a boil; reduce heat and simmer 2 minutes. Add the Worcestershire sauce and half-and-half and season with salt and pepper. Remove from the heat and stir in the lemon juice.

Place the hot toast on 4 warm plates and spoon the mushrooms on top. Serve immediately.

4 servings

Asparagus and Cheese Soufflé Omelet

1 package (10 oz)
  frozen asparagus,
  thawed
6 eggs, separated
2 tablespoons water
Salt and pepper
1 cup grated sharp
  Cheddar cheese
2 tablespoons butter

Reserve a few asparagus spears for garnish. Coarsely chop the remainder.

Beat 3 egg yolks with 1 tablespoon of the water in a bowl and season with salt and pepper. Stir in ½ cup of the cheese and half of the chopped asparagus. Beat 3 egg whites until very stiff. Fold into the egg yolk mixture.

Melt 1 tablespoon of butter in an 8-inch omelet pan. Pour in the omelet mixture and spread evenly in the pan. Cook over a low heat for 5 minutes, until golden brown underneath. Transfer the pan to a hot broiler and broil for 1 minute, until the omelet is puffy and lightly browned on top.

Slide the unfolded omelet onto a warmed plate and make a second omelet with the remaining ingredients. Garnish with the reserved asparagus.

4 servings

Corn Fritters with Bacon

2 tablespoons flour
1 egg, separated
Salt
Cayenne pepper
1 can (12 oz) whole
    kernel corn
12 slices bacon
Oil for
    shallow-frying

Beat the flour and egg yolk together in a small mixing bowl. Season with salt and cayenne. Add the liquid from the corn and mix well. Stir in the corn. Beat the egg white until stiff; fold into the batter. Cook the bacon; keep warm.

Add oil to a depth of ½ inch to a large skillet and heat. Drop in spoonfuls of the batter. Brown on one side, then turn and brown the other side. Drain on paper towels and serve immediately with the bacon.

4 servings

Toad in the Hole

1 lb pork sausages
½ cup milk
½ cup water
2 eggs
1 cup all-purpose
  flour
Salt

Arrange the sausages in a greased 12 ×
7½ × 2-inch ovenproof dish. Bake in a
425° oven for 10 minutes.

Combine the remaining ingredients
in a blender and whirl to mix.

Reduce the oven temperature to
400°. Pour the batter over the sausages
and bake for 25 to 30 minutes, until
well risen and golden brown.

4 servings

Tuna Gougère

⅔ cup water
5 tablespoons butter
⅔ cup plus 1
  tablespoon flour,
  sifted
Salt and pepper
2 eggs, beaten
½ cup grated
  Cheddar cheese
1 onion, chopped
⅔ cup vegetable or
  chicken broth
⅔ cup milk
2 ripe tomatoes,
  peeled and
  chopped
1 can (7 oz) tuna,
  drained and flaked
1 tablespoon grated
  Parmesan cheese
1 tablespoon fresh
  bread crumbs

Combine the water and 4 tablespoons
of the butter in a medium saucepan
and bring to a boil. Remove from the
heat and quickly beat in ⅔ cup of the
flour. Season with salt and pepper and
beat vigorously until the mixture is
smooth and comes away from the side
of the pan. Cool slightly. Beat in the
eggs, a little at a time. Stir in the
cheese. Spoon the mixture around the
side of a greased 8-inch pie plate.

Melt the remaining tablespoon of
butter in a large skillet. Add the onion,
and sauté until softened. Stir in the
remaining flour and sauté 1 minute.
Gradually stir in the broth and milk
and simmer, stirring, until thickened.
Add the tomatoes and tuna and season
with salt and pepper.

Spoon the mixture into the pie plate
and sprinkle with the Parmesan and
the bread crumbs. Bake in a 400° oven
for 30 to 40 minutes, until well risen
and golden brown.

Serve hot, garnished with chopped
parsley.

4 servings

Onion Tart

PASTRY:
- 2 cups all-purpose flour
- ½ teaspoon salt
- 4 tablespoons butter
- 4 tablespoons shortening
- 1 to 2 tablespoons water

FILLING:
- 4 tablespoons butter
- 1½ lb onions, sliced
- ¼ lb fatty smoked bacon, chopped
- ¼ cup flour
- ⅔ cup sour cream
- 3 eggs, lightly beaten
- ½ teaspoon salt
- ½ teaspoon pepper

Prepare and roll out the pastry as for Quiche Lorraine (see opposite), cutting in the shortening with the butter.

To make the filling, melt the butter in a large skillet. Add the onions and bacon, and sauté until soft and golden, but not browned. Remove from the heat and stir in the flour, sour cream, eggs, salt and pepper.

Pour the mixture into the prepared pastry shell and smooth the top. Bake in a 400° oven for 35 to 40 minutes, until set and golden brown.

6 servings

Quiche Lorraine

PASTRY:

2 cups all-purpose
  flour
½ teaspoon salt
⅔ cup butter
1 to 1½ tablespoons
  water

FILLING:

½ lb bacon, partially
  cooked
3 eggs
⅔ cup whipping
  cream
Pepper

Sift the flour and salt into a large mixing bowl. Cut the butter in and work with a fork until the mixture resembles fine crumbs. Add the water and mix to a firm dough. Knead lightly until smooth. Wrap in plastic wrap or waxed paper and chill for 15 to 20 minutes.

Roll the dough out on a lightly floured board into a 10-inch round and use to line a 9-inch pie pan. Crimp edges and trim away excess pastry. Prick the base with a fork and chill for 20 minutes.

Line the pastry shell with the bacon slices and bake on the top shelf of a 400° oven for 10 minutes.

Beat the eggs and cream together lightly and season with pepper. Pour into the bacon-lined pastry shell and return to the oven for 25 to 30 minutes, until set and golden brown.

6 servings

Mushroom and Pepper Pizzas

PIZZA BASE:
2/3 cup milk
1/2 cup butter
2 packages dry yeast
3 eggs, beaten
4 cups all-purpose
   flour
1 teaspoon salt

PIZZA TOPPING:
2 tablespoons oil
2 onions, chopped
2 cans (14 1/2 oz each)
   whole tomatoes
2 cloves garlic,
   minced
1 small bay leaf
1 teaspoon each
   dried basil and
   oregano
Salt and pepper

TO FINISH:
1/4 lb mushrooms,
   sliced and sautéed
   in butter
1 green pepper,
   sliced

Heat the milk and butter in a small saucepan until warm. Remove from the heat, stir in the yeast and blend well. Beat in the eggs.

Sift the flour and salt together in a large bowl. Stir in the yeast and milk mixture and mix to a smooth dough. Cover with a damp towel and let rise in a warm place for 45 minutes.

Meanwhile, prepare the topping. Heat the oil in a large skillet. Add the onions and sauté gently until softened. Add the tomatoes with their juice, the garlic and herbs and season with salt and pepper. Bring to a boil; reduce the heat and simmer for 20 minutes, stirring occasionally, until the sauce is thick. Let cool.

Turn the dough onto a floured board and cut into 4 pieces. Roll each piece out into an 8-inch round and place on a greased baking sheet.

Spoon the topping over the top of the 4 pizzas. Sprinkle the mushroom and pepper slices on top. Cover and leave in a warm place to rise for 10 minutes.

Bake in a 450° oven for 35 to 40 minutes, until firm and golden brown.

Makes four 8-inch pizzas

Ham Pizzas

4 Pizza Bases
Pizza Topping
   (opposite page)
¼ lb cooked ham,
   chopped
24 black olives

Place the pizza bases on baking sheets
(see directions for making opposite).
    Combine the basic pizza topping in
a mixing bowl with the ham and
olives. Spoon over the pizzas. Let rise
and bake as directed opposite.
Makes four 8-inch pizzas

Anchovy Pizzas

4 Pizza Bases
Pizza Topping
   (opposite page)
½ lb Cheddar
   cheese, sliced
2 cans (2 oz each)
   anchovy fillets

Place the pizza bases on baking sheets
(see directions for making opposite).
    Spoon the topping over the pizzas.
Cover each with a layer of cheese and
arrange the anchovies on top. Let rise
and bake as directed opposite.
Makes four 8-inch pizzas

Rustic Pie

PASTRY:

2 cups all-purpose flour

Salt

¾ cup butter

Squeeze of lemon juice

1 to 1½ tablespoons water

FILLING:

3 eggs, beaten

1½ cups ricotta or small-curd cottage cheese

1 cup grated Parmesan cheese

1 onion, chopped

2 tablespoons chopped chives

Salt and pepper

1 tablespoon oil

2 cloves garlic, minced

1 can (14½ oz) crushed tomatoes

1 tablespoon tomato paste

4 tablespoons dry white wine

½ teaspoon each dried marjoram and oregano

¼ lb black olives, pitted

½ lb mozzarella cheese, sliced

1 green pepper, seeded and thinly sliced

Prepare the pastry as for Quiche Lorraine (see page 77), adding the lemon juice with the water. Cover and chill for 30 minutes.

Meanwhile, prepare the filling. Combine the eggs, ricotta and Parmesan cheeses, onion and chives in a mixing bowl. Season with salt and pepper and blend well.

Heat the oil in a large skillet. Add the garlic and sauté for 1 minute, without browning. Stir in the tomatoes, tomato paste, wine and herbs and season with salt and pepper. Bring to a boil and simmer rapidly for about 15 minutes, until thickened. Let cool.

Divide the pastry in half. On a lightly floured board, roll out one piece to a 10-inch round and use it to line a 9-inch pie plate.

Spread half the cheese mixture evenly over the bottom of the pastry shell. Sprinkle half the olives over the top and arrange half the mozzarella slices over them. Spoon in half the tomato sauce and arrange the pepper slices on top. Repeat the layering with the remaining ingredients. Roll out the remaining pastry and cover the pie. Seal and flute the edges and make 3 or 4 diagonal slashes through the top. Bake in a 425° oven for 35 minutes, until golden brown.

Let settle for 30 minutes before serving.

6 to 8 servings

French Bread Pizzas

1 loaf French bread
1 can (4 oz) tomato
   puree
1 to 2 teaspoons
   dried mixed herbs
1 to 2 cloves garlic,
   minced (optional)
4 tomatoes, sliced
¼ lb sliced salami
8 slices lean bacon
2 tablespoons capers
1 cup grated Gruyère
   cheese

Cut the bread in half lengthwise and spread each half generously with the puree. Sprinkle with the herbs and garlic.

Arrange the tomato and salami slices on each piece. Lay the bacon slices on top and sprinkle with the capers and the grated Gruyère.

Cut each half in four pieces. Place on a lightly greased baking sheet. Bake in a 400° oven for 15 minutes. Serve hot.

4 to 8 servings

Spanish Eggs

4 tablespoons oil
2 slices day-old
   bread, cubed
2 potatoes, diced
1 onion, chopped
1/4 lb bacon, chopped
1/8 lb green beans, cut
   into 2-inch
   lengths
6 tomatoes, peeled,
   seeded and
   chopped
2 zucchini, thinly
   sliced
8 thin slices garlic
   sausage, diced
4 eggs

Heat the oil in a 10-inch skillet. Add the bread and fry until browned. Remove the croutons from the skillet and drain on paper towels.

Add the potatoes to the skillet and sauté for 15 minutes, until browned. Add the onion and bacon and sauté for 2 minutes. Stir in the beans, tomatoes and zucchini and sauté for 5 to 7 minutes. Stir in the sausage.

Transfer to a large shallow oven-proof dish and make 4 hollows in the mixture with the back of a spoon. Break an egg into each hollow. Bake in a 350° oven for 12 minutes. Sprinkle the croutons over the top and bake for 3 minutes.

4 servings

Eggs Provençale

Double recipe
   Mayonnaise
   (page 62)
3 to 4 cloves garlic,
   finely minced
2 to 3 teaspoons
   tomato puree
6 hard-cooked eggs

Thoroughly blend the mayonnaise with the garlic and tomato puree.

Cut the eggs in half lengthwise and arrange on six lettuce-lined salad plates. Cover with the mayonnaise mixture and chill. Serve garnished with strips of pimiento and black olives.

6 servings

Deviled Eggs

6 hard-cooked eggs
4 tablespoons
   mayonnaise
1 clove garlic,
   minced
1 teaspoon curry
   powder
1/2 teaspoon prepared
   English mustard
1/2 teaspoon tomato
   puree

Cut the eggs in half. Remove the yolks and force through a sieve. Add the mayonnaise, garlic, curry powder, mustard and tomato puree and blend to a smooth, soft paste. Pipe or spoon the mixture into the egg whites. Arrange on a serving plate and garnish with the watercress and chives. Sprinkle paprika or cayenne over the top.

4 to 6 servings

Alsace Sausage Crepes

CREPE BATTER:

1 egg

1 cup milk

1 cup all-purpose
  flour

¼ teaspoon salt

2 tablespoons butter,
  melted

FILLING:

½ to ¾ lb cooked
  Polish sausage,
  thinly sliced

1½ cups grated
  Gruyère cheese

2 tablespoons
  chopped parsley

½ green onion,
  minced

1 clove garlic,
  minced

Combine the egg, milk, flour and salt in a blender and whirl until smooth. Refrigerate for 2 hours, or until ready to use. Add the melted butter and mix well.

Lightly oil an 8-inch crepe pan or skillet and heat until very hot. Pour in enough batter to barely cover the pan, and tilt to distribute evenly. When the edge begins to brown, cover with one-sixth of the sliced sausage and sprinkle with ¼ cup of the grated cheese. Place under a hot broiler for 20 to 30 seconds until the cheese melts. Slide the unfolded crepe onto a plate and keep warm while preparing the remaining crepes.

Mix the parsley, green onion and garlic and sprinkle over the crepes.

6 servings

Potato Pancakes

1 lb potatoes, grated
   into cold water
1 onion, grated
2 eggs, lightly beaten
¼ cup flour
¼ teaspoon grated
   nutmeg
Salt and pepper
Oil for frying

Drain the grated potatoes thoroughly and combine with the onion. Toss together, then drain again in a colander, pressing with the back of a spoon to remove any excess water.

Turn into a mixing bowl, add the eggs, flour and nutmeg and season with salt and pepper. Mix well.

Heat a little oil in a 12-inch skillet until sizzling. Drop the potato batter into the skillet by teaspoonfuls and spread out flat with the back of a spoon. Sauté over moderate heat for 4 to 5 minutes, until crisp and golden underneath. Turn with a spatula and sauté the other side until golden.

Keep hot while making the remaining pancakes. Serve hot.

Makes about 15 pancakes

Cottage Cheese Blintzes

FILLING:
1 lb dry-curd cottage cheese
2 egg yolks, beaten
3 to 4 tablespoons sugar
⅛ teaspoon salt
⅛ teaspoon cinnamon
1 to 2 tablespoons milk

BLINTZES:
½ cup flour
¼ teaspoon salt
2 eggs, lightly beaten
¾ cup milk
1 tablespoon melted butter
1 to 2 tablespoons butter

Combine the cottage cheese, egg yolks, sugar, salt, cinnamon and milk in a mixing bowl and blend together well, adding more milk if necessary.

Sift the flour and salt into a mixing bowl. In a separate bowl mix the eggs, milk and 1 tablespoon melted butter together. Add to the flour and beat until smooth.

Brush the bottom and side of a 6-inch skillet with a little melted butter and heat until a bead of water "dances" on the surface. Using about 2 tablespoons of batter for each blintz, spoon into the hot skillet, tilting the skillet to distribute the batter evenly. Brown lightly on one side, about 30 seconds, and turn out onto a paper towel, browned side up. Cook the remaining blintzes in the same manner.

Place about 1½ tablespoons of the filling in each blintz. Fold the bottom up and the sides in over the filling; roll up. Melt the remaining butter in a skillet and sauté the blintzes until warmed through. Serve hot with sour cream and fruit.
Makes 12 blintzes

Apple Fritters

½ cup all-purpose flour
1 egg, separated
¼ cup water
1 teaspoon oil
Oil for frying
2 large apples, peeled, cored and cut in ¼-inch rings
Powdered sugar

Beat the flour, egg yolk, water and oil well. Beat the egg white until stiff and fold into the batter.

Pour oil to a depth of 1 inch into a large heavy skillet and heat until hot. Dip the apple slices in the batter, letting the excess drip off, and carefully slide into the hot oil. Fry for 2 to 3 minutes, until golden.

Drain on paper towels and sprinkle heavily with powdered sugar. Serve hot with cream.
4 servings

Chicken Liver Vol-au-Vents

1 package (10 oz)
    pastry shells
2 tablespoons butter
1 lb chicken livers,
    chopped
1 onion, chopped
2 mushrooms,
    chopped
1 tablespoon flour
⅔ cup chicken broth
1 tablespoon grated
    Parmesan cheese

Bake the pastry according to package directions. Meanwhile, melt the butter in a skillet. Add the chicken livers and sauté gently for 3 to 4 minutes, until lightly browned. Remove from the skillet.

Add the onion to the skillet and sauté until softened. Add the mushrooms and sauté for 1 to 2 minutes. Stir in the flour, then the broth. Simmer, stirring, for about 5 minutes. Remove from the heat and stir in the chicken livers.

Remove the "lids" from the pastry shells and spoon the filling into the shells. Sprinkle with the cheese. Replace the lids and serve.

6 servings

Whole Wheat Croustades

1 can (7 oz) tuna, drained
1 stalk celery, finely chopped
1 tablespoon stuffed green olives, chopped
1 hard-cooked egg, chopped
3 tablespoons mayonnaise or salad dressing
2 green onions, chopped
1 tablespoon chopped parsley
Lemon juice
8 large slices day-old whole wheat bread
¼ cup melted butter

Combine the tuna, celery, olives, egg, mayonnaise, green onions and parsley in a mixing bowl and season with a squeeze of lemon juice.

Trim each piece of bread into a large circle and brush liberally with the melted butter. Fit into 8 cupcake pans, shaping up the sides. Bake in a 350° oven 30 to 45 minutes, until very crisp and golden brown. Remove from the pans and cool on racks.

Spoon the filling generously into each toast cup and garnish with sliced stuffed olives.

4 servings

Turkey Blanquette

2 tablespoons butter
3 tablespoons flour
1½ cups turkey or
  chicken broth
8 slices cooked
  turkey
1 egg yolk
2 tablespoons cream

Melt the butter in a small saucepan and stir in the flour. Cook, stirring, for 1 minute. Remove from the heat and gradually stir in the broth. Return to the heat and simmer, stirring, for 1 to 2 minutes. Cool.

Arrange the turkey in a shallow baking dish. Spoon the sauce over the turkey. Cover with foil and bake in a 375° oven for 25 minutes, until hot.

Beat the egg yolk and cream in a cup and blend a little of the hot sauce into it. Stir the mixture into the baking dish and return to the oven for 3 minutes.

Serve garnished with chopped parsley if desired.

4 servings

Chicken and Nut Sandwiches

2 cups diced cooked
  chicken
2 stalks celery,
  chopped
¼ cup chopped
  cucumber
2 green onions,
  chopped
¼ cup bean sprouts
2 tablespoons
  mayonnaise
2 tablespoons
  chopped peanuts
1 tablespoon
  chopped parsley
Lemon juice
4 pita breads
8 lettuce leaves
2 tomatoes, sliced

Combine the chicken, celery, cucumber and green onions in a bowl. Stir in the bean sprouts, mayonnaise, peanuts and parsley and season with a squeeze of lemon juice.

Warm the pita breads. Cut each in half and open to form a pocket. Place a lettuce leaf in each pocket. Spoon in the chicken salad and top with a slice of tomato.

4 servings

Deluxe Chicken Sandwiches

4 slices white bread,
  crusts removed
2 tablespoons
  mayonnaise
4 slices buttered
  brown bread,
  crusts removed
2 teaspoons Dijon
  mustard
8 slices cooked
  chicken
3 tomatoes, sliced
Salt and pepper
4 lettuce leaves

Spread the white bread with the mayonnaise and the brown bread with the mustard. Lay the sliced chicken on the brown bread. Top with tomato slices and season well with salt and pepper. Place the lettuce on top and finish with a layer of white bread. Press together gently and cut into quarters.

4 servings

Double Decker Ham Sandwich

½ cup minced ham
1 teaspoon prepared
  mustard
2 tablespoons
  mayonnaise
1 package (3 oz)
  cream cheese with
  chives
8 slices brown bread
4 tomatoes, sliced
4 lettuce leaves,
  shredded
4 slices buttered
  white bread

Mix the ham, mustard and mayonnaise together in a small bowl.

Spread cream cheese on four slices of the brown bread. Top with the sliced tomatoes. Spread the remaining brown bread with the ham mixture and place on top of the tomatoes, ham side up. Sprinkle with the shredded lettuce and top with a slice of white bread.

Press down gently and cut each sandwich in quarters.

4 servings

Crabmeat Sandwiches

1 can (6½ oz)
  crabmeat
Lemon juice
1 to 2 tablespoons
  mayonnaise
1 tablespoon
  chopped parsley
2 tablespoons
  chopped chives
Salt and pepper
8 slices buttered
  brown bread,
  crusts removed
Chopped watercress

Combine the crabmeat with a squeeze of lemon juice, the mayonnaise and herbs in a mixing bowl and season with salt and pepper. Mix well.

Spread the mixture generously over 4 slices of the bread. Top with the chopped watercress and lay the remaining bread slices on top. Cut in quarters.

4 servings

INDEX

Almond soup, chilled, 35
Anchovy pizzas, 79
Apple fritters, 86
Asparagus and cheese
    soufflé omelet, 72
Avocado soup, iced, 34

Bean
    kidney, and artichoke salad,
      56
    salad, mixed, 43
    salad with salami, 57
    soup with pistou, 26
Beef stock, 6
Blintzes, cottage cheese, 86
Brown rice salad, 45

Carrot soup, cream of, 30
Cauliflower salad, 39
Celery and apple salad, 40
Cheddar log with salad, 55
Cheese and onion soup, 13
Cheese soufflé, herbed, 71
Chestnut soup, puree of, 14
Chicken
    and nut sandwiches, 91
    sandwiches, deluxe, 92
    soup, creamy, 10
    stock, 6
Chicken liver vol-au-vents,
    88
Chinese cabbage salad, 40
Coleslaw with yogurt dressing,
    44
Corn fritters, 73
Corn soup, cream of, 14
Cottage cheese blintzes, 86
Crabmeat sandwiches, 93
Crepes, Alsace sausage, 84
Croustades, whole wheat, 89
Cucumber and yogurt soup, 28
Cucumber soup, minted, 32

Eggplant and crabmeat soup,
    17

Eggs
    deviled, 83
    Provençale, 83
    Spanish, 83
    with vegetable hash, 66

Fennel soup, 10
Fish stock, 6
French dressing, 63
Fritters
    apple, 86
    corn, with bacon, 73
Fruit salad, hot, 61

Garlic soup, 16
Garnishes for soup, 7
Gazpacho, 29
Gougère, tuna, 75
Green herb dressing, 63

Ham
    pizzas, 79
    sandwich, double decker, 92
    soufflé omelet, 70

Kidney bean and artichoke
    salad, 56

Lentil and tomato salad, 47
Lentil soup, 20
Lima bean
    and cauliflower salad, 47
    salad, 40
    soup, puree of, 24
    vinaigrette, 58

Mayonnaise, 62
Melon, tomato and grape salad,
    59
Minestrone, main meal, 8
Mint and honey dressing, 64
Mulligatawny soup, 22
Mushroom(s)
    and bean sprout salad, 38
    and pepper pizzas, 78
    creamed, on toast, 72
    soup with Madeira, 9
Mussel chowder, 19